Happy Coloring!

Heather Land

HEATHER'S ADULT COLORING BOOKS

www.HeatherLandBooks.com

THIS BOOK
BELONGS TO

_____

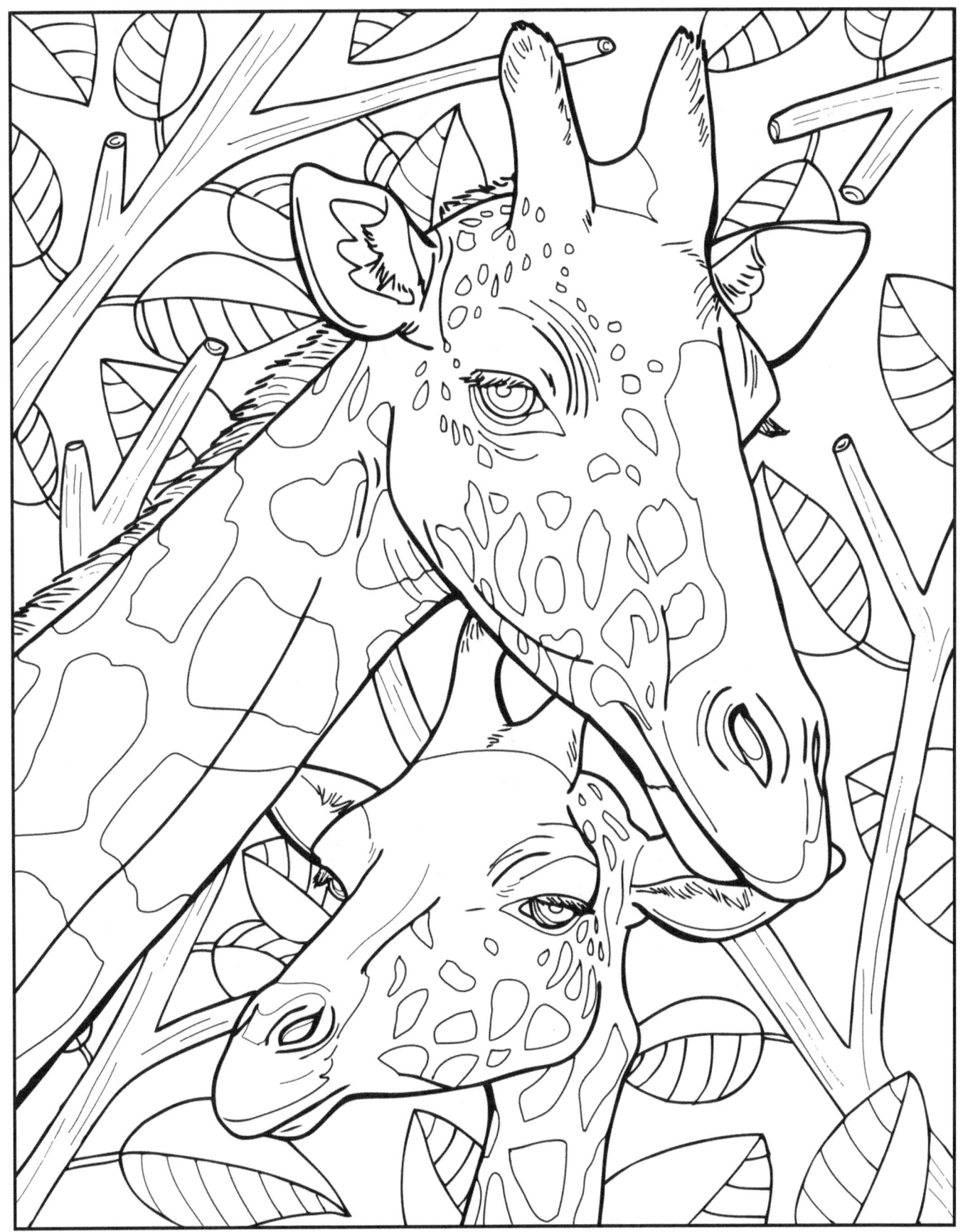

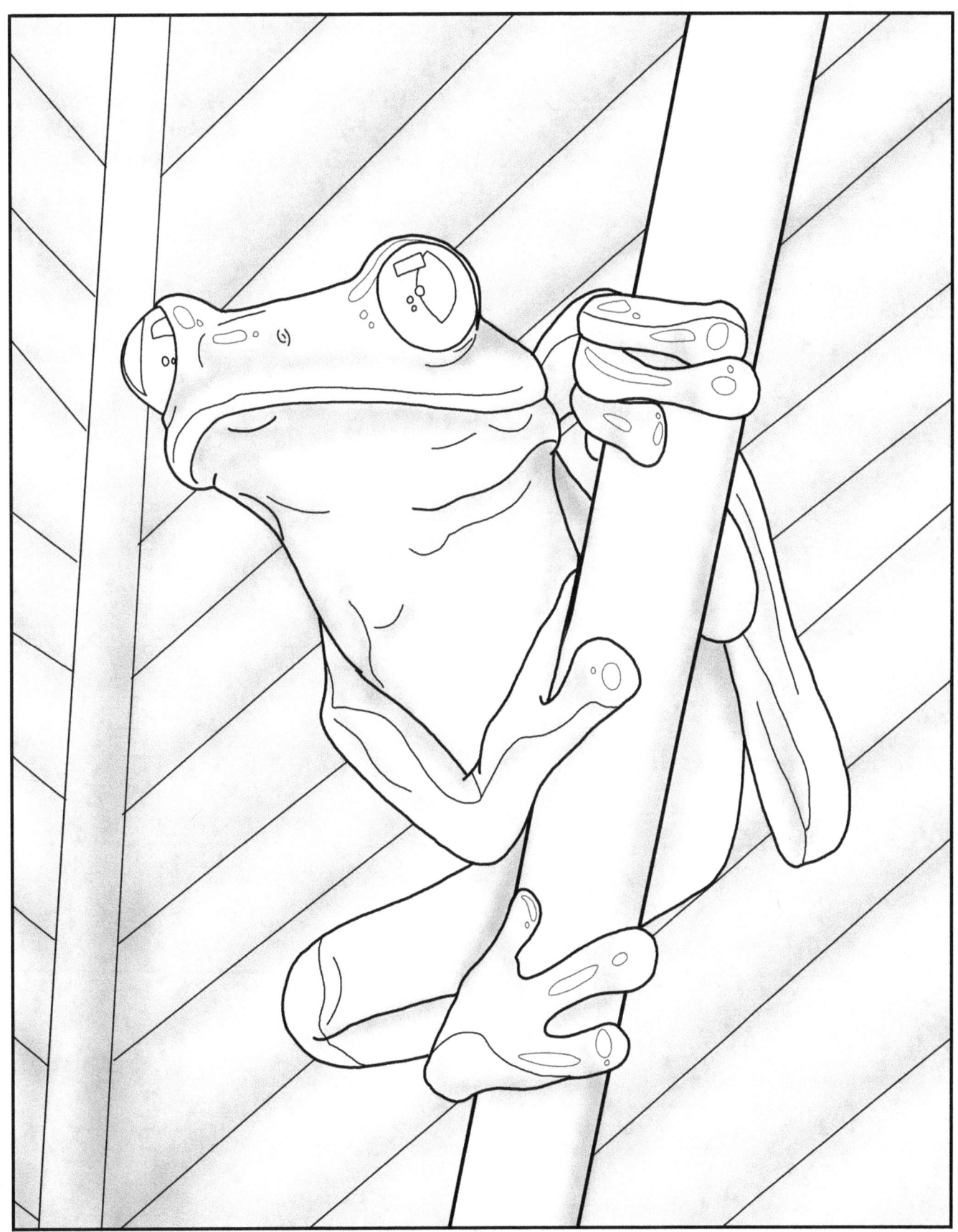

COLOR TEST SQUARES

TEST YOUR COLORS HERE AND USE THIS
PAGE AS A REFERENCE GUIDE

COLOR TEST SQUARES

TEST YOUR COLORS HERE AND USE THIS
PAGE AS A REFERENCE GUIDE

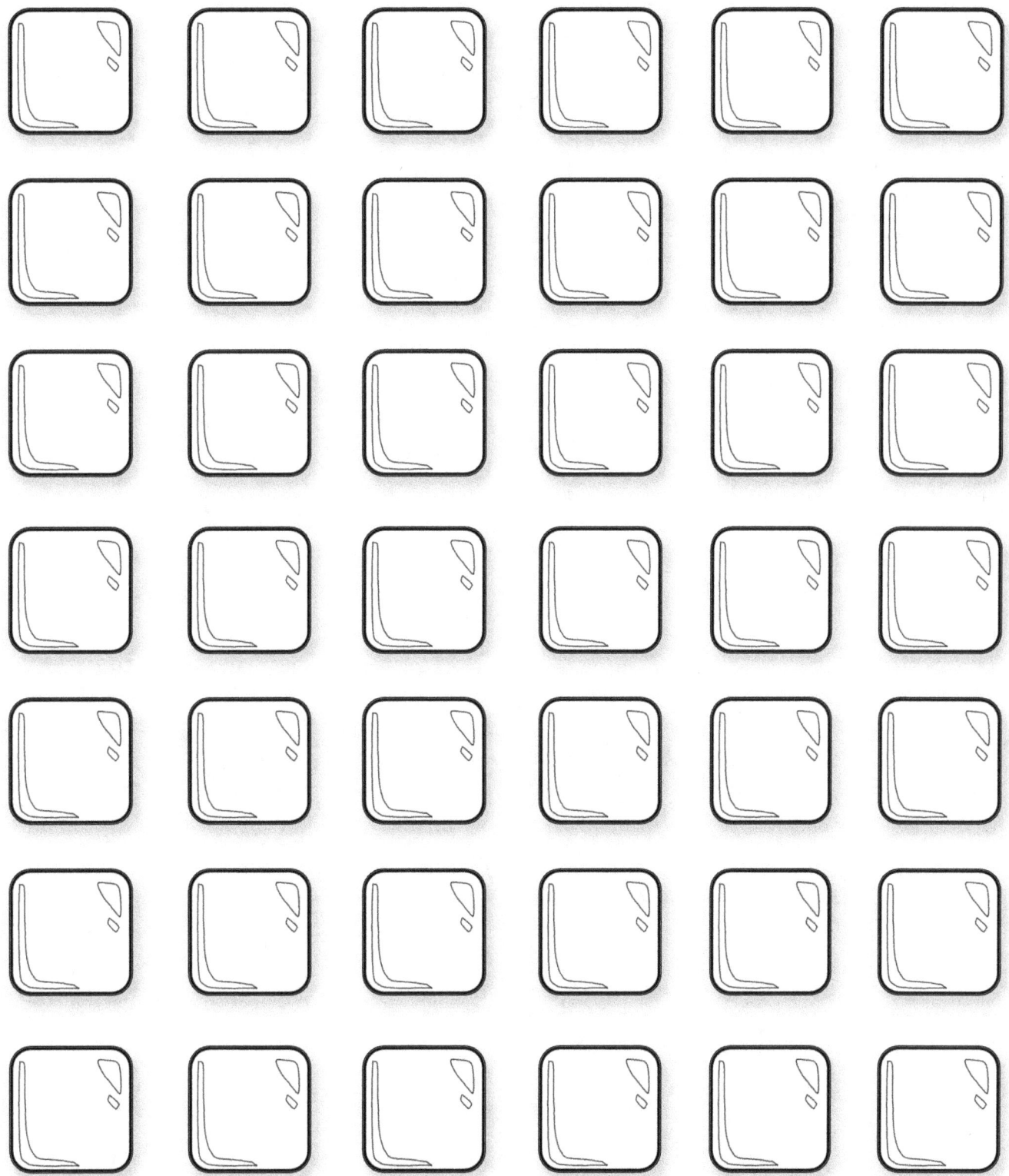

www.ingramcontent.com/pod-product-compliance
Lightning Source LLC
Chambersburg PA
CBHW081416280526
45788CB00009B/3123